THE LAW of SEED

Your Seed And Your Destiny

The Law Of Seed

All Rights Reserved

Copyright © 2016 by Sampson Amoateng

No part of this publication may be reproduced, stored in a retrieval system or transmitted in any way by any means, electronic, mechanical, photocopy, recording or otherwise, without the prior written permission of the author except as provided by USA copyright law.

All Bible references are taken from the New King James Version, unless otherwise stated.

Author's Contact: *amoatengsampson1@yahoo.com*

The opinions expressed by the author are not necessarily those of Rehoboth House.

EBook: 978-1-60796-933-4
Paperback: 978-0996426770
Hardcover: 978-0996426787

Printed in United States of America

Published by Rehoboth House, Chicago, USA
rehobothhouseonline.com

Table Of Contents

Dedication..ix

Acknowledgment..xi

Introduction..xiii

Chapter 1
Different Kinds Of Seeds...1-30

Chapter 2
Gifts And Talents...31-36

Chapter 3
Strategic Relationship..37-42

Chapter 4
Destiny Helpers And Destiny Killers....................43-48

Conclusion..49-54

Prophetic Prayer Declaration...................................55-56

Dedication

I dedicate this book to my beloved parents, Dr. Gabriel Amoateng-Boahen *(Former Chaplain, University of Chicago Hospital)* and Mrs. Agatha Amoateng-Boahen *(CEO Maranatha Hospital)*, House of Miracle *(HOM)* members globally, and to all partners of Sampson Amoateng Ministries.

Dedication

Acknowledgement

Most importantly, I thank the Almighty God, our Heavenly Father for His immeasurable grace and love towards me, and for giving me the insight to write this book, and be a blessing to His people. Father, indeed, if it had not been for your mercies extended to me, I wouldn't have been who I am today. I humbly say thank your sir, in Jesus' name. Amen.

I thank my parents Dr. and Mrs. Gabriel Amoateng-Boahen for nurturing me in the fear of the Lord and guiding me through life from cradle to maturity. The impact you made in the lives of my siblings and I, is evident today. We couldn't have had better parents. I am proud of you and will ever remain grateful to God. Thank you mom and dad.

I thank all my spiritual mentors, especially, Apostle John Abercrombie of Truth & Deliverance International Ministries headquartered in Chicago, my covenant brother, Apostle Danjuma Musa of Global Flame Ministry, Jos, Nigeria, for their selfless support and impact in my life and ministry.

I also use this opportunity to thank all members of House of Miracle Ministries (HOM) and partners of Sampson Amoateng Ministries, around the globe. Your support has been a formidable source of strength and encouragement to me.

Finally, I thank all those who have impacted me in one way or the other, whose names I have not mentioned. My heart says thank you to all of you.

Introduction

It is imperative to understand that God's Kingdom operates according to the spiritual laws He set in motion. Interestingly, these laws are replete in His written word.

The Kingdom of God is not subject to the limitations of natural laws. It is a supernatural kingdom with supernatural abilities far above the laws of nature. Supernatural simply means superior to the natural.

One of the laws of the Kingdom this book will discuss is "The Law of Seed". Understanding the dynamics of this law and how it functions is imperative to accomplishing great feats and fulfilling God's purpose for our lives. The law of seed is the hub that governs the productivity of man on earth.

Therefore, in order to receive anything from God, we must understand that there are laws governing the operation of the kingdom of God and willingly align ourselves with them.

Introduction

Nevertheless, so often we attempt to circumvent these spiritual laws, hoping to obtain the promises therein even when we fail to obey them as required. Unfortunately, the violation and ignorance of these laws have kept many in the Body of Christ in perpetual toiling from hand to mouth and from one form of affliction to another. If you are in such cycle of defeat, I believe the Lord has allowed this book "The Law of Seed" in your hands to reverse that ungodly sequence and give you a pleasant story to tell.

With every emphasis, God will never violate the spiritual laws He has established that govern the operation of His kingdom and the entire universe. We must agree with the fact that these universal laws of the kingdom are what regulate life in its entirety.

The perfect work of redemption accomplished on the Cross of Calvary by Jesus Christ our Lord qualifies us to access these divine provisions made accessible to us by God.

The Law of Seed

I have come to realize by experience, both in ministry and real life, that the primary reason why most believers are living below the level of prosperity and quality of life God intended is because of lack of understanding of the dynamics of the laws and principles of the Kingdom of God. Consequently, this anomaly has led to a high rate of believers living unfulfilled lives.

God, in His infinite wisdom, divinely made man in three distinct components; the spirit, the soul and the body. Oftentimes, it is said that man is a spirit, has a soul and lives in a body.

> *"Now may the God of peace Himself sanctify you completely; and may your whole spirit, soul, and body be preserved blameless at the coming of our Lord Jesus Christ. He who calls you is faithful, who also will do it" (1 Thessalonian 5:23).*

God created man in this order for a purpose. Therefore, in order for us to experience the best of life as designed by God, we must understand the functionalities of these distinct components of man in our everyday life and what God intended for them to accomplish. God, in His infinite wisdom, planned the total wellbeing of man through these components to enable man maximize his God-given potential. No part of these three components should be neglected, otherwise, we suffer the consequence.

The Body

The body is the outer part of man that houses the soul and the spirit. It is material in nature and through it we function in this material world. Our body contains our nervous system with nerves and the brain. With our body we interact with the physical world through our five physical senses; smell, feel, touch, taste and see. As I have said earlier, it is commonly said that man is a spirit, has a soul and lives in the body.

The Soul

Our soul has three major components; our mind, our will and our emotion. It is our soul that gives us our personality and through it we live out our relationship with God and man. Our mind has a conscious part and a subconscious part. The conscious mind is where we do our thinking and reasoning. The sub-conscious mind is where we hold our deep beliefs, our attitudes and also retain our memories. Our emotion is where we have and express our feelings. Our will is what gives us the ability to make choices and take decisions.

The Spirit

It is through our spirit that we have communion and fellowship with God. It is our spirit that gives us intuition between right and wrong. At the deepest level our human spirit is where we derive the meaning and purpose of life. It is our real self.

Having said that, in most cases we fail to pay adequate attention to these three aspects of man. Consequently, a greater percentage of us live far below the level of prosperity and quality of life God intended for us to experience.

Introduction

"His divine power has given us everything we need for life and godliness through our knowledge of him who called us by his own glory and goodness" (2 Peter 1:3).

As you diligently read and apply the principles enunciated in this book with faith in your heart, you will be better positioned for a positive change in your life. It is imperative to know that there is a seed strategically positioned in you by the power of the Holy Ghost. If that seed is adequately harnessed, it empowers you to fulfill God's plan for your life and experience the fullness of life. That seed represents the particular thing God wants you to accomplish in your lifetime.

CHAPTER 1

DIFFERENT KINDS OF SEEDS

Different Kinds Of Seeds

There are different kinds of seeds God gave to humanity. We are going to specifically examine the seeds that can potentially enable us to live a fulfilled and accomplished life. Perhaps you have never considered time, effort, action, talents and gifts as seeds. The seed of time, the seed of effort, the seed of action and the seed of talents and gifts are potentials that can propel us to the greatest height of accomplishment if adequately harnessed.

According to the Cambridge dictionary a seed is a small, round, or oval object produced by a plant and from which, when it is planted on the ground, a new plant can grow. The process by which seeds become plants is called "germination." Inside of every seed is an embryonic plant waiting for the right conditions to present themselves. Until that time, the seed remains dormant. Some seeds can remain dormant for years and still be viable. God gave man seed for the purpose of planting. After the seed is planted, it goes through a process in order to germinate and produce fruits.

> *"And God said, Behold, I have given you every herb bearing seed, which [is] upon the face of all the earth, and every tree, in the which [is] the fruit of a tree yielding seed; to you it shall be for meat" (Genesis 1:29).*

There is a seed strategically positioned in every Christian by the power of the Holy Ghost. If it's well harnessed, it enables you to fulfill God's plan for your life. Each seed represents a particular thing that God wants you to accomplish in life. The more this seed is put to profitable use, the more harvest it produces. The target of the enemy is to destroy that divine seed in you. According to the scriptures, Jesus is the seed of the woman that was designated to bruise the head of Satan and restore everything that man lost when Adam fell.

> *"And I will put enmity between you and the woman, and between your seed and her Seed; He shall bruise your head, and you shall bruise His heel" (Genesis 3:15).*

When angel Gabriel visited Mary, he told her that she shall have a seed. That seed was Jesus, who came at the fullness of time.

> *"But when the fullness of the time had come, God sent forth His Son, born of a woman, born under the law" (Gal 4:4).*

The enemy in the person of King Herod attempted to kill the seed, even as a baby. He was very desperate in his pursuit of eliminating the seed that he ordered the massacre of every male child within the age of two in Bethlehem. He left no stone unturned in his desire to destroy the seed and terminate God's program for Jesus and humanity at large. However, by the wisdom of God, the seed was preserved while the enemy was permanently defeated and bruised.

> *"Then Herod, when he saw that he was deceived by the wise men, was exceedingly angry; and he sent forth and put to death all the male children who were in Bethlehem and in all its districts, from two years old and under, according to the*

time which he had determined from the wise men"
(Matthew 2:16).

Your seed is your next level, your seed is your prosperity, and your seed is everything that God has designed and arranged for you. He has set the law of seed time and harvest in motion that guarantees a harvest after sowing.

"As long as the earth exists seedtime and harvest, and cold and heat, and summer and winter, and day and night shall not cease" (Genesis 8:22).

There are no shortcuts to harvest. Neither is there a substitute for sowing. The only way to stand in faith for a harvest is to act in accordance with the word of God and sow. According to scriptures, we shall reap in proportion to our sowing.

"He that sows little shall reap little; and he which sows generously shall reap generously" (2 Corinthians 9:6).

The Seed of Time

Time is a valuable seed and a currency in this part of the universe. It is a force of nature and a tangible entity created by God. It plays a very deep role in our fundamental physical theories. With it we can measure events from the past to the present and even into the future. If time is channeled productively, we can accomplish great and memorable things that can outlive us. Time should not be squandered; rather, it should be used wisely and productively. If time is used efficiently, we can reap its maximum benefit.

"To everything there is a season, a time for every purpose under heaven: (Eccl 3:6).

Everything God created, even the heavens and the earth, functions with time. God uses time to accomplish His plans for man and everything that exists on earth. He used six days to create the universe and rested on the seventh day, and afterwards He declared that everything that He spent time to create was good and perfect.

> *"Then God saw everything that He had made, and indeed it was very good. So the evening and the morning were the sixth day" (Gen 1:31).*

God gave man time so we can effectively plan our daily lives. I am going to outline some of the ways we can use the seed of time to accomplish significant purpose in life. Time is money, and anything that is set to waste your time will profit you nothing and should be avoided at every instance.

> *"While the earth remains, seed-time and harvest, and cold and heat, summer and winter, day and night shall not cease" (Gen 8:22).*

The Seed of Time in Education

Formal and informal education play a key role in building a successful life worth living. Your seed of time invested in education generally could be rewarding. As we pass through the corridors of the formal educational system, from preschool through to universities, we acquire a wealth of knowledge after studying a specific area of specialization. Informal education coupled with real life lessons we experience daily can also provide understanding and knowledge of specific fields of discipline.

Conclusively, the seed of time invested in education has become the primary means of livelihood for many in our modern society around the globe today. This helps in building our professional life based on what we set our hearts to do.

Through the seed of time sown in education, we decide the future career path for our lives. This decision could be influenced by our passion and desire for a particular discipline, like being a doctor, a nurse, a lawyer, an engineer, a teacher, etc. It could also possibly be influenced by other external factors. We in turn reap the benefits of our education as we are paid for the professional services we provide or product we make. Education is key in fostering social mobility and reducing the burden of poverty. The more educated we are, the higher the chances of experiencing a successful career and a glorious and fulfilling future.

The Seed of Time in Work

Work is an integral aspect of man. The seed of work is one of the assignments given to man at creation by God.

> *"Then the Lord God took the man and put him in the Garden of Eden to tend and keep it" (Gen 2:15).*

All diligent work deserves a reward. The result of work comes in form of wages or payments, which typically rewards our efforts invested in the work. Time efficiently invested as a seed in work generates profitable results. As believers, the Word of God instructs us to work because the hands that does not work shall not eat.

"For even when we were with you, we commanded you this: If anyone will not work, neither shall he eat" (2 Thessalonian 3:10-11).

It is the desire of our heavenly Father that we become successful and productive in every aspect of our lives as we diligently work, in most cases as means of livelihood. Whatever your profession is, God is pleased when your work brings harvest. Through the seed of work, God wired us to be fruitful and productive in life.

First and foremost, a trained doctor owes a legal duty of care to patients. He is required to administer treatment to sick patients and ensures that the right prescription drugs to facilitate recovery are administered. Consequently, the doctor discharging his duties is expected to receive his reward for the time sown in taking care of the patient. It is expected that whatever work we have been called or assigned to do, we do it diligently in order to receive the benefit of the seed of time sown into that work.

"Whatever your hand finds to do, do it with all your might, for in the realm of the dead, there is neither working nor planning nor knowledge nor wisdom" (Ecclesiastes 9:10 NIV).

The Seed of Time in Ministry

To devote your life to ministry requires adequate preparation through the knowledge of our Lord Jesus Christ and the specific assignment He has commissioned you for. This is characterized by spending time in mentorship, learning and observing the doctrines of the Church as you prepare to lead God's people. You need to invest between five to ten years in order to build a solid ministry. Ministry is not laying hands on people to fall on the ground or a means of power display. True ministry is to make people follow you as you follow Christ and guide them to conform to the image of Christ. Ministry is modeling the life of Christ that will compel people to follow Christ because of your lifestyle. Ministry is being an extension of God's blessings to humanity at large.

Efficient use of your time in respect to work, education and ministry goes a long way towards giving you the wealth and resources you need to stay happy and live a fulfilled life. Conversely, the inefficient use of your time with respect to work, education and ministry will in turn lead to a life of despair, frustration and unproductive. In fact, it's a recipe for stagnation and failure. The Bible states clearly that we should be careful how we use the seed of time given to us in whatever endeavor of life and ensure that we make the best use of it.

> *"And say to Archippus, "Take heed to the ministry which you have received in the Lord, that you may fulfill it." (Col 4:17).*

For example, anyone who responds to the divine call to ministry, with full assurance of the promises of God for his life, is able to endure hardness in the ministry in difficult and challenging times. Even if going through a seemingly helpless time of rejection and opposition by people around you who do not believe in the ministry God has called you into, you do not despair. Those early stages in ministry you invested in gathering a few members to start prayer meeting sessions will never go unrewarded. Though it might be small in the eyes of man at the moment, in due time it will spring up. Surely as the Lord lives, the ministry will survive and fulfill the agenda of heaven on earth.

As you read this book, I prophecy over that ministry God has entrusted to your stewardship, remain focused on His word and promises; He will surely bring into fruition what He has promised you. As it is written, *"I will watch over my words to perform them."* The Lord will give you the strength and grace needed in order for you to build and sustain that ministry in Jesus' name. Amen

Seed of Effort

Effort is the use of physical, mental or spiritual energy needed to achieve something. It is a

Different Kinds Of Seeds

vigorous and determined attempt we make to accomplish a feat. Every effort you make in life either to work or upgrade yourself in any endeavor will certainly one day bring tangible results that will be evident to all. The greater the effort, the greater the achievable results. Effort also represents hard work, dedication and commitment to whatever you find yourself doing, which consequently results in possession of something that one can boost of.

> *"He that sows little shall reap little; and he which sows generously shall reap also generously"* (2 Corinthians 9:6).

Some Christians are expecting to reap where they have not sown, while others are expecting to reap generously when they have sown sparingly. This is a violation of the divine laws of the Kingdom of God. I call it self-delusion or living in ignorance of the Kingdom's principles. It is clearly stated in the scriptures above that you reap in proportion to what you sow.

The Law of Seed

The Word of God clearly states that if we want a continual and generous harvest, we should sow continually and generously despite whatever state we are currently in. We will never change our circumstances until we begin to operate according to the law of the seed of effort.

This is one of the core reasons why most believers don't see the promises of God manifested in their lives. Again and again they attempt to 'stand in faith' and 'believe God' for a generous harvest - yet they have never sown the amount of seed necessary to obtain that level of harvest.

Too often they hear teachings on the blessings of divine prosperity as promised in the word of God and they endeavor to stand in faith and believe God for prosperity; good. But unfortunately they fail to follow biblical instructions on how to obtain that level of prosperity, which simply comes by continually sowing faithfully and generously.

Different Kinds Of Seeds

Most people develop an attitude after they worked hard and things did not turn out as they anticipated. To some, they conclude that the principles doesn't work or they can't do it again. Therefore, there is no need to make a second attempt. Unfortunately, in doing so, they faint and the promises of God never manifest in their lives because they slipped back on the decision to hold fast to what they wanted to accomplish.

> *"And let us not be weary in well doing: for in due season we shall reap, if we faint not" (Galatians 6:9).*

The more effort you put in, the more inner zeal and passion you have to purposefully engage in your work. In order to reap what you have sown with hard work and perseverance, you have to be steadfast.

> *"Therefore, my beloved brethren, be steadfast, immovable, always abounding in the work of the Lord, knowing that your labor is not in vain in the Lord" (1 Corinthians 15:58).*

The Law of Seed

> *"Let us hold fast the profession of our faith without wavering; (for he is faithful that promised ..." (Hebrews 10:23).*

If you take a closer look at life, everything emanated from a seed; trees, flowers, birds, animals, fish and even you.

> *"While the earth remaineth there will be seedtime and harvest, and cold and heat, and summer and winter, day and night shall not cease" (Genesis. 8:22 KJV).*

Money was invented by man as a means of exchange of goods and services as civilization continued. But it represents the fruit of our labour. The seed of effort is connected to your harvest and the harvest applies to money too. The Bible says this also applies to money. This principle is confirmed in Galatians 6:7: *"Do not be deceived, God is not mocked for whatever a man sows, that he will also reap."*

The more your effort, the bigger your results. But if your effort is weak your results will be correspondingly weak. It is important that believers work with all their might in order to achieve uncommon results leading to successful Christian living. As a believer, the diligently you work, the more results you get from the work done. Your input is going to determine your output in life. If you put less effort into accomplishing that bigger task your vision will be impaired, as you will not have a clear picture of your results because your effort was minimal. In this life, nothing comes easy; you need to work above the regular by the wisdom of God to be able to outwit the system of the world and have outstanding results.

Don't think like those who have allowed the challenges of life place limitations on them. Always go the extra mile by diligently putting in more effort to the work wherein you have been assigned to. Trust and depend on the wisdom of God as you concentrate more on God in prayer and fasting. This supernatural dimension will surely give you an edge over others. I can assure you that as you apply this kingdom principle you will receive the best out of your pain.

Many people believe the concept of sowing and reaping, but fail to recognize the law of the seed of effort working in their everyday life. The seeds of your effort and the diligent work you have sown determine what you get in return. The seed of effort connects you to your harvest. The kind of seed you sow determines the kind of harvest you will reap. For example, if a farmer sows corn seeds, he is sure to receive a harvest of corn. Likewise, when you sow God's word into your heart, you shall inevitably reap His promises accordingly.

Your seed of effort is to rid yourself from the spirit of laziness and procrastination. Unfortunately, some Christians procrastinate, as a result they fail to put God's word to work. It is interesting to know that only those who act on the word shall be blessed.

Different Kinds Of Seeds

"But he who looks into the perfect law of liberty and continues in it, and is not a forgetful hearer but a doer of the work, this one will be blessed in what he does" (James 1:25).

Seed of Action

Newton's 3rd Law states that, "for every action there is equal but opposite reaction." Paul said *"whatsoever a man sows he reaps."* Whatever kind of lifestyle you live has an effect on your children and even on generations after them. If you sow a good seed, you reap a good harvest. But if you sow mischievously you shall reap commensurately what you've sown. Your seed of action is evident in your expected harvest. Guard and protect the seed planted so that they grow to your expectation. Your lifestyle as a believer is a reflection of the training you received and the process you go through to arrive at your destination.

Even though in life there may be ups and downs and things may not have gone the way you anticipated, as you read this book the Lord's grace is abundantly released over your life for you to accomplish that set goal you have in mind. It's not too late to revisit those dreams God planted in your heart. God is always standing at the finishing line waiting for you to cross the line and enter your rest. He may not be there when you think you need Him, but I can assure you, God is never late. Just in the nick of time, He shows up.

If you watch athletes closely when running a race, they exert sufficient energy to enable them to finish the race well. Every competitor is looking to receive the prize at the end of the race. But amongst all the competitors only one will eventually win the ultimate prize. They all started on the same line, at the same time, on the same command and on the same rules and regulations governing the race. No one is favored above the others. The whistle is blown once for them all to set off the race. The harder you press towards outracing your opponent, the greater your chances of winning the race. The winner knows the amount of energy he requires that enhances his chances of winning the race. The loser always knows that he did not put in much effort in order to win the prize. Laziness and procrastination potentially impede our passion to accomplish our goals and vision in life.

> *"Then Isaac sowed in that land, and received in the same year a hundredfold: and the Lord blessed him" (Genesis 26:12 KJV).*

There is a story of a mentally demented man who wanders about seeking for food. One day he went to a woman he usually gets food from and she gave him a poisoned loaf of bread. The mentally ill man decided not to eat the bread immediately. As he wandered away from the woman, he saw little children returning from school and gave part of the poisoned bread to some of them. Unfortunately, one of the children he gave the poisoned bread to was that woman's child. The innocent child ate the poisoned bread and died. This woman reaped the seed of her action.

Jesus said in Luke 6:31 *"And just as you want men to do to you, you also do to them likewise."* If you throw a ball to the wall, it bounces back to you. This stands to attest to the fact that whatever a man sows, he reaps. Your seed of action will give you what you deserve. When you enlarge your coast towards achieving your priorities in life and exert more diligence in all action, you have a broader coverage of what you stand to achieve and you reap the result of your actions. "The more action the more the results; the lesser the action the lesser your results."

Seed of Talent

Talent is an inbuilt skill that naturally helps someone to do somethings without struggle. It's a natural ability or aptitude endowed by God at birth. It enables one to do somethings without exerting much effort. There are different types of talents. There are talents of dancing, playing football, boxing, basketball, music, etc. It is an ability that someone is born with. Talents are gifts from God that, if wisely used, can earn you money, fame and popularity. Examples of people who have used their talents profitably include Mike Tyson (Boxer), Ronaldo (Football player), Michael Jackson (Musician, Dancer) Mr. Bean (Comedian) and Michael Jordan (Basketball player). These few people affected the world in their respective disciplines by using their talents beyond making money. They impacted lives in diverse ways, motivating younger generation to take up the challenge to use their gifts and talents positively to do something meaningful in life.

A famous Ghanaian comedian and actor wrote behind his car, like a bumper sticker "the benefit of comedy." By wisely using his talent he has experienced upward social mobility. He is now a celebrity and a role model for many young people.

God endows us with various talents through genetic transfer to serve His purpose and be a blessing to others. Each of us has something to give. We can give our money, our time and our skill. We can extend our compassion to the sick and be a friend to the lonely. We can volunteer to be peacemakers, teachers or ministers and also for charity works.

The Apostle Paul Phrased It This Way:

> *"We have different gifts, according to the grace given us. If a man's gift is prophesying, let him use it in proportion to his faith. If it is serving, let him serve; if it is teaching, let him teach; if it is encouraging, let him encourage; if it is contributing to the needs of others, let him give generously; if it is leadership, let him govern diligently; if it is showing mercy, let him do it cheerfully"* (Romans 12:5-8 NIV).

In His Parable of the Talents, the Lord Jesus taught us to use our gifts wisely. A talent was a very large sum of money, about 80lb/36 kg of silver. Before embarking on a journey,

Different Kinds Of Seeds

a wealthy man entrusted his fortune to his servants for the time he would be away. Two of the servants used the money wisely to earn income for their master. However, the third servant did not put the money into productive use. When the master returned to take stock of their stewardship, he was displeased with the servant who failed him.

> "Again, it will be like a man going on a journey, who called his servants and entrusted his property to them. To one he gave five talents of money, to another two talents, and to another one talent, each according to his ability. Then he went on his journey. The man who had received the five talents went at once and put his money to work and gained five more. So also, the one with the two talents gained two more. But the man who had received the one talent went off, dug a hole in the ground and hid his master's money.
>
> "After a long time the master of those servants returned and settled accounts with them. The man who had received the five talents brought the other five. 'Master,' he said, 'you entrusted me with five

talents. See, I have gained five more.' His master replied, 'Well done, good and faithful servant! You have been faithful with a few things; I will put you in charge of many things. Come and share your master's happiness!'

"The man with the two talents also came. 'Master,' he said, 'you entrusted me with two talents; see, I have gained two more.' His master replied, 'Well done, good and faithful servant! You have been faithful with a few things; I will put you in charge of many things. Come and share your master's happiness!'

"Then the man who had received the one talent came. 'Master,' he said, 'I know that you are a hard man, harvesting where you have not sown and gathering where you have not scattered seed. So I was afraid and went out and hid your talent in the ground. See, here is what belongs to you.' His master replied, 'You wicked, lazy servant! So you knew that I harvest where I have not sown and gather where I have not scattered seed? Well then, you should have put my money on deposit with the bankers, so that when I returned I would have received it back with interest.'

"'Take the talent from him and give it to the one who has the ten talents. For everyone who has will be given more, and he will have an abundance. Whoever does not have, even what he has will be taken from him. And throw that worthless servant outside, into the darkness, where there will be weeping and gnashing of teeth" (Matthew 25:14-30 NIV).

The master represents God in this parable, and the servants represent us. The English word talent is derived from this parable. It is fitting because the lesson of the parable is for us to understand that the responsibility to use our talents and wealth in God's service rests on us.

If we do not use our gifts wisely, God will regard us as wicked and lazy like the unprofitable servant in the parable.

Serving the need of others brings meaning and fulfillment to our lives, in ways that wealth, power, possessions and self-centered pursuit can never bring.

The Law of Seed

"As Jesus said, give, and it will be given to you. A good measure, pressed down, shaken together and running over, will be poured into your lap. For with the measure you use, it will be measured to you" (Luke 6:38 TNIV).

It seems as if the more we give to others the poorer we become, but just the opposite is true!

"There is one who scatters, yet increases more; And there is one who withholds more than is right, but it leads to poverty. The generous soul will be made rich, and he who waters will also be watered himself" (Proverbs 11:24-25).

Different Kinds Of Seeds

CHAPTER 2

GIFTS AND TALENTS

Gifts And Talents

There is a difference between natural talent and supernatural gift. Talent is our number one asset that is genetically inherited. It runs through our genes. It is a potential that must be harnessed or else it remains dormant. Without proper training, you can't maximize your talent. For your talent to be reckoned with and attain success, it must be cultivated and uniquely expressed. Everyone has unique talents and abilities. Conversely, spiritual gifts are directly given by the Lord to accomplish a divine purpose that will benefit mankind and advance the course of God on planet earth. It is a supernatural empowerment from the Lord that gives us the privilege to partner with divinity here on earth.

Paul wrote:

"Now there are varieties of gifts, but the same Spirit; and there are varieties of services, but the same Lord; and there are varieties of activities, but it is the same God who activates all of them in everyone. To each is given the

manifestation of the Spirit for the common good"
(1 Corinthians. 12:4-7 NRSV).

He further mentioned some of the gifts that were given to the early Christians for the purpose of building the Church.

"To one is given through the Spirit the utterance of wisdom, and to another the utterance of knowledge according to the same Spirit, to another faith by the same Spirit, to another gifts of healing by the one Spirit, to another the working of miracles, to another prophecy, to another the discernment of spirits, to another various kinds of tongues, to another the interpretation of tongues. All these are activated by one and the same Spirit, who allots to each one individually just as the Spirit chooses"
(1 Corinthians 12:8-11 NRSV).

In His description of the final judgment in Matthew 25, Jesus made it crystal clear that we will be judged on our response to the needs of others. It does not matter the magnitude of our talents. What matters to God primarily is how we utilize the talents (seeds) that are given to us to make an impact in our generation.

Gifts And Talents

"From everyone to whom much has been given, much will be required; and from the one to whom much has been entrusted, even more will be demanded" (Luke 12:48 NRSV).

DIFFERENCE BETWEEN TALENTS AND GIFTS

TALENTS	GIFTS
Talents are genetically inherited from our parents at birth, as natural endowments.	Gifts are spiritually received from God at new birth, as supernatural endowments.
Talents are possessed both by the saved and the unsaved. There are many talented unsaved people.	Gifts are possessed only by born again believers in the Lord Jesus Christ. The unsaved can only mimic spiritual gifts.
A person may be talented as an outstanding teacher, possibly being envied by fellow teachers for his compelling communication skill and oratory.	Conversely, if this person receives the gift of teaching at new birth, it will be distinct from his previous teaching abilities. Spiritual gifts are determined by God, not by our natural talents and abilities.

Gifts And Talents

Talents possessed by believers ought to be surrendered and consecrated to the Lord and used for His honor and glory. Example, a skilled organist playing as unto the Lord.	Gifts are given by God for the outworking of God's life as expressed by the Body of Christ. When the Body is healthy the life of God is manifested and God is glorified *(1 Corinthians 14:24-25)*.
If you are naturally talented, you must undergo training to develop your talent and become proficient. Oftentimes, it can be very demanding. Example, most professional athletes not only have talents, they developed their talents through years of rigorous practice and hard work sustained by constant discipline.	Gifts are exercised by faith, as the believer stays spiritually healthy, growing in the grace and knowledge of the Lord Jesus Christ. Spiritual growth and maturity are required to exercise them. "... *Of the knowledge of the Son of God, to a perfect man, to the measure of the stature of the fullness of Christ"* *(Ephesians 4:13).*

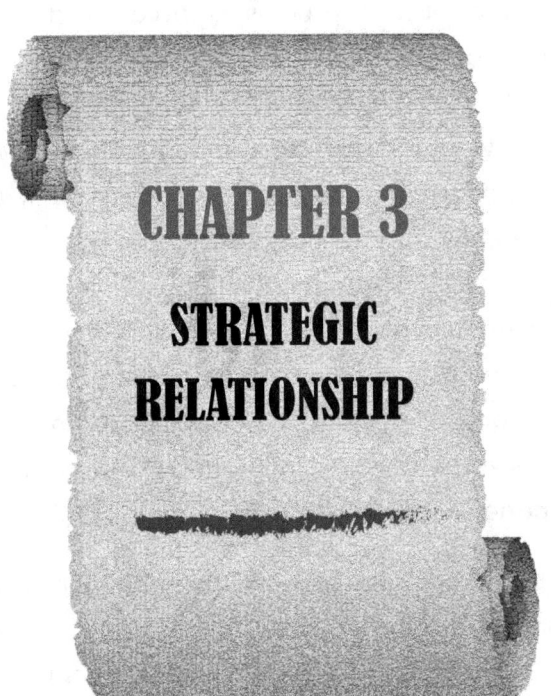

CHAPTER 3
STRATEGIC RELATIONSHIP

Strategic Relationship

Building strategic relationship is a key factor in accomplishing great things in life. It is an important part of the learning and development process required at different stages of our lives. Strategic relationship is about being sensitive to available resources and leveraging them to accomplish what God has assigned you to do. It provides you with the opportunity to learn from those who have gone ahead of you in life and gives you access to connect with people of substance that have what you need to move upward to the next level of accomplishment. Most importantly, it gives you access to a mentor and his wealth of experience that you can leverage.

Take some time to envision what strategic relationship means for you and how it would help you to accomplish the goals you have set in the next three to five years. What would the next phase of your career look like? Do you desire to become a man or woman of God with a unique anointing, or an entrepreneur, a leader, a board member, an expatriate working in a foreign country? It's up to you and what God has put in your heart. The answers to these questions will help you think more strategically on how to make the most of your time in building strategic relationships. This kind of relationship can influence you positively to remain focused and resolute when the going gets tough, and to pay whatever price required to fulfill your vision.

When you have a precise and definitive vision that is measurable, strategic planning will help you focus on issues that are relevant in accomplishing that vision. You will have no time for frivolities. Every seed of time for you at such times counts and matters a lot.

Also, think of strategy as a systematic approach in your life that would enable you to accomplish specific goals within a specific time-frame. For example, if you want to be a successful business person or a servant of

God with global recognition, who is positively impacting lives, your key strategy would be to connect yourself to such business people and servants of God who will act as fathers and mentors to you. This strategic relationship would surely sharpen and streamline your life, and give you a direction and purpose to live for. As for me, one of my pathways to achieve this plan would be to seek their advice and connect with them by reading their books and listening to their messages in order to learn what made them successful in their respective fields of discipline.

This seed of strategic relationship will go a long way towards impacting us and giving us a clear picture of the road-map to our life's journey. It would streamline our lifestyle and better position us to experience prosperity in what we have planned to accomplish, and consequently fulfill God's purpose for our lives. By so doing, our seed of spending quality time to connect with such people of influence will in turn remold, refine and position us better in life to reach our desired destination.

Not having a road-map or a clearly defined route in life is a recipe for stagnation, setbacks and frustration. The enemy's assignment is to strip you of the blessings of God by luring you off track with the distractions of life. But as you read this book and align yourself with these Kingdom principles enunciated in it, you stand a better chance of triumphing over every evil wish against you, designed to truncate the purpose of God for your life. As God strategically strengthens your relationship with these people, He releases divine help that will propel you into your promised land.

Saul went in search of his father's lost donkey in 1 Samuel 9 and got connected to Prophet Samuel. That relationship eventually led him to finding the lost donkey. In other words, after Samuel anointed Saul, the higher anointing of Prophet Samuel that came upon Saul brought a restoration of what was lost.

Strategic Relationship

"When you leave me today, you will meet two men near Rachel's tomb, at Zelzah on the border of Benjamin. They will say to you, 'The donkeys you set out to look for have been found" (1 Sam 10:2-3).

By divine arrangement, after leaving the presence of Prophet Samuel, two strangers were strategically positioned to give Saul the good news about the lost donkey, which was his assignment at the time.

Your seed of strategic relationship causes God to send these helpers into your life. These people are strategically positioned to help you accomplish God's divine purpose for your life.

CHAPTER 4
DESTINY HELPERS AND DESTINY KILLERS

Destiny Helpers And Destiny Killers

Life is about God linking you with your destiny helpers. There are two kinds of people you will ever meet in life. 'Destiny Helpers' and 'Destiny Killers.' When God links you with your destiny helpers, your tears will be converted to joy, your torment to peace, your labour to favour, your pain to gain and your Goliath becomes your stepping stone to the place of celebration.

No man can by himself fulfill his destiny. Everyone needs a destiny helper. Even if you are an Elisha you need your Elijah. Joshua needed his Moses, Timothy needed his Paul. Even Jesus needed John the Baptist to introduce Him. He had twelve destiny helpers (disciples) who promoted His destiny. These twelve helpers were strategically positioned and called by God in order to fulfill His plan to reconcile man and creations back to Himself through His son Jesus Christ. Notice that Jesus did not walk alone.

"And by Him to reconcile all things to Himself, by Him, whether things on earth or things in heaven,

having made peace through the blood of His cross. And you, who once were alienated and enemies in your mind by wicked works, yet now He has reconciled" (Col 1:20-22).

'Destiny Killers'

Destiny killers are those who never expect or believe that anything good can come out of your life. Oftentimes they say it verbally as well with their attitude and actions. Destiny killers always see the negative side of you and are constantly making an effort to discourage you. Joseph's brothers thought they would end his life in the pit, but God sent a man to get him out of the pit and take him to the land where he was destined to be a Prime Minister (Genesis 37:1-33).

You have to learn how to discern destiny killers and avoid sharing your goals with them. They will always discourage and distract you from your goal. Whoever you share your future plans with and he makes you feel discouraged and inadequate to pursue that goal is a potential destiny killer. Avoid telling such people what God has put in your spirit to accomplish. They can quench your light and the zeal necessary to pursue your vision. Joseph's brothers were typical examples of destiny killers.

'Destiny Helpers'

Destiny helpers are motivators. Whenever you discuss with them about what God is doing in your life, they encourage you and make you feel like mounting up with wings like the eagles. They are always there to push you beyond your limits, because they understand that with God on your side, you can accomplish even greater goals. They are more concerned about your potential than your limitations. They major on your positives and minor on your negatives. They are like Barnabas the son of encouragement.

> *"But Barnabas took him and brought him to the apostles. And he declared to them how he had seen the Lord on the road, and that He*

had spoken to him, and how he had preached boldly at Damascus in the name of Jesus" (Acts 9:27-28).

God will not physically come down and help you. He will send people to you, so be alert to discerning their presence in your life. When you meet them, your life will move from zero to hero. They are agents of change, agents of transformation, agents of elevation, agents of enlargement, agents of promotion and agents of uncommon breakthrough. Your destiny helpers are strategically positioned to help you arrive at your expected end.

4 Things That Can Happen to Your 'Destiny Helpers'

- They can be killed.

- They can be missed by you.

- They may not show up at all, through your lifetime.

- They can be hidden from you, through the manipulations of the powers of darkness.

I counsel you to say this prayer daily:

"O Lord make me visible to all my destiny helpers and invisible to every destiny killer, in Jesus' name. Amen."

Conclusion

God gives seed to the sower and bread to the eater. The more you sow, the more you harvest. If these seeds are sown wisely you will reap a bountiful harvest. But if you waste your seed, you will have no harvest to reap in return.

At times it amazes God when we complain and ask Him to give us everything we could ever need, including money, a wife, house, cars, or jobs, just to mention a few. The truth is that God has given us everything that pertains to life and godliness in the form of seed. Our responsibility is to translate those seeds into tangible resources by wisely deploying them profitably.

Laziness goes a long way towards retarding and impeding our growth as believers. A lazy person will always revolve around a problem rather than finding a solution to it. A farmer has to cultivate the soil where the seed is planted in order for the roots to get the requisite nutrients it needs from the ground.

The Law of Seed

If the farmer is lazy and fails to do what is required to ensure that the seed grows and yields its fruit, his harvest will fall short of his expectations. He could possibly even lose his harvest. A careful use of your seed will give you the results you need in life.

In a nutshell, every seed God placed in you as a believer goes a long way towards transforming your life holistically, as you pursue your purpose in life. A prudent use of these seeds will give you the ministry, the money, the good health, the marriage, the career, the family and every other good thing that God has promised us as believers. If we can cautiously guard our lives according to how His word demands, it will help us to attain the best that God has designed for us as believers.

It is interesting to know that every miracle Jesus performed in the Bible was a collaboration of the divine and the human. He will pray and ask the person to take an action in order to experience the miracle.

Conclusion

And a certain man was there which had an infirmity thirty and eight years. When Jesus saw him lie, and knew that he had been now a long time in that case, he saith unto him, wilt thou be made whole? The impotent man answered him, Sir; I have no man, when the water is troubled, to put me into the pool: but while I am coming, another steppeth down before me. Jesus saith unto him RISE, TAKE UP THY BED AND WALK. Immediately the man was made whole, and took up his bed, and walked: and on the same day was the Sabbath day"
(John 5:5-9. KJV).

The essence of life is worshiping God, obeying His word and helping others. God has given each of us the specific seed and gift required to fulfill His purpose for our lives. Like the three men we read about earlier in Jesus' Parable of the Talents, our gifts may either be great or small. Regardless the size of our talents, abilities and wealth, we are required to put them to profitable use.

I pray that as you read this book, the Lord will cause every seed He deposited in you to bear tangible fruits in your life and bring you the peace, joy and prosperity divinely assigned to you as a Christian, in Jesus' name. Amen.

"For I know the thoughts I think towards you, saith the Lord, thoughts of peace and not of evil to give you an expected end" (Jeremiah 29:11 KJV).

Conclusion

PROPHETIC PRAYER DECLARATION

- *Any evil red light that stops my seeds from growing, I quench you in Jesus' name. Amen*

- *Any evil man or woman, who has vowed that I will not see my harvest this year, I disarm and nullify all your evil decrees, and render them void, in Jesus' name. Amen.*

- *Any power that always attacks my destiny helpers; be disgraced by fire in Jesus' name. Amen.*

- *Any evil night farmer who has been assigned to uproot my seeds sown, be exposed and be destroyed by fire, in Jesus' name. Amen.*

- *Every evil power chanting and calling my name in any demonic mirror and crystal ball, die, in Jesus' name. Amen.*

- *Every evil mouth anointed to curse me be sealed up, in Jesus' name. Amen.*

Prophetic Prayer Declaration

- *Oh, God arise and let all satanic orchestrated problems in my life die, in Jesus' name. Amen.*

- *Oh, God arise and let my story change for better, in Jesus' name. Amen.*

- *Oh, God silence all my silencers, in Jesus' name. Amen.*

- *Oh, Lord, let me see fruitfulness in my ministry, career, education, family, and in all aspect of life, in Jesus' name. Amen.*

- *I move from every form of slavery to ultimate freedom in Christ, in Jesus' name. Amen.*

- *I move from every form of insult to undeniable results, in Jesus' name. Amen.*

www.ingramcontent.com/pod-product-compliance
Lightning Source LLC
Chambersburg PA
CBHW052135010526
44113CB00036B/2261